Finding Your Interest

Terms and Conditions

Table Of Contents

Foreword

A lot of us meander through life not truly recognizing what we were meant to accomplish. Rather than coasting through life without placing your finger on how to discover your passion in this world, attempt to pinpoint what that passion is. Get all the info you need here.

Discovering Your Passion

Developing Your Life by Pinpointing Your Passion

Chapter 1:

Passion For Life Basics

Synopsis

A few tips to get you started with the basics in getting some passion back into your life.

The Basics

Attend to yourself. When you start paying attention to your body, and its well-being, things will come to you. By standing up off the sofa and running or walking on a day-to-day basis, it may get your blood pumping and your brain working. Pay attention to your ideas as you work out, and a few invigorating things might pop up.

Take heed with your inner child. If there was a huge dream you held onto while growing up, attempt and determine why you relinquished it. As youngsters we have no obligations, and that leads us to daydream. As we become older, a few of these daydreams get put on the back burner for grownup obligations. They may be brought to the forefront again.

Look for help. Your acquaintances and loved ones will be able to help you recognize what you are great at, and what a few of your hopes and aspirations are. By connecting to these individuals, and requesting direction, you might discover answers.

Put down ideas. Writing may be a great way to see on paper a recurring theme(s). Finding out a secret wish or goal may be hard, however if you really listen to what your joys are, you may simply discover a passion in life.

Voluntary work. By stepping outside of yourself, and assisting other people, you may recover some of the joy that you seek. Assisting the elderly may be an awesome way to hear about their marvelous lives and may spark off an interest that you don't presently think about. It may be hard to discover a passion in life, however never quit trying.

Get going. Once you have a few thoughts that interest you, get out and attempt to get moving in a new career or interest. By taking classes, or internships or a new job, you may discover out if what you are really passionate about.

Chapter 2:

Your Surroundings

Synopsis

There are a lot of factors which may play into your success at touching base with your inner passion and originative thinking. The want to discover precisely what you wish from your life is just the opening move.

Your Surroundings

Working out how to dig out those long entombed passions and interests is a different story. If you're setting about the job of producing a vision board you might discover yourself taking steps that will open you up mentally and let you relax and feel originative in order to discover those inner wants.

Meditation, music and pictures may inspire you once you start your vision board; however a different thing that you might not have thought about is your surroundings. Originative surroundings may inspire your passions.

Whether you're most pleased in a neutral room with passive colors and décor or choose brilliant, vibrant items surrounding you, you may discover what originative surrounding works better for inspiring you by doing some experimenting. This is like trying out assorted kinds of music to determine which relaxes you most.

Inside and out you may take the time to sit in a couple of different spaces, encircled by different items to discover out what makes you experience something. Relaxation is great, but the urge to accomplish something is even greater.

Whether your environment makes you want to sing or take a photo, draw or compose or just sit and dream the idea is to discover the paragon place for you to connect with your inner self.

A few individuals connect with themselves while they're unwinding; other people need some stimulant in order to stir their originative juices. Regardless what kind of surroundings work for you the theme is to open your brain to all the possibilities and move into a place where you may see yourself working toward a goal of some kind.

Once you think of originative surroundings you might feel that in order to be originative you ought to be surrounded by artworks however originative environments aren't only about the décor, it's about how it makes you feel.

So if your originative place is sitting on a limb in the woods hearing the birds whistle, or in a window seat with sunshine streaming in, that's fantastic. It's all about you and how your place makes you feel.

Even if you are not making a vision board it's crucial to spend some time in an originative place so that you may stay in touch with your inner passions and originative thinking. This conducts a more balanced mental attitude and less tension in your life.

Chapter 3:

Expand Your Mind

Synopsis

Have you ever desired to have a carefree, passionate and fun-loving personality, however felt it wasn't "you", or were upset about the implications?

There's a way to have an originative, cheerful life-style with plenty of happiness and meaning in life and yet be a responsible individual.

Expand Your Brain

It begins with believing and trying fresh things. That simple? Well, it doesn't all occur overnight, but it may start overnight, and go along for the rest of your life if you wish.

In order for your life to enlarge, your brain needs to expand. Simply like with exercising, once you urge your muscles, they grow. It's the same with your brain; once you think or try fresh things, your brain expands. And an extended brain is an enriched brain. You become enriched, and so does your life story.

It may lead to passion in life, an extroverted personality; you meet fresh interesting individuals, try fresh fun things, and build self-assurance and self-regard, which all bring you happiness and meaning in life.

How do I put together a passionate life, an extroverted personality? How do I meet fresh interesting individuals, try fresh fun things, build confidence and self-regard, and finally find happiness and a meaningful life?

There are a number of ways to expand your believing and actions in daily life. Trouble is that occasionally we discover ourselves "in a rut" that we simply can't seem to get out of.

What is more, we have a disposition to put on our autopilot and carry out the motions in our lives, without consciously believing about what's going on around us.

Have you ever been pressing home from work or school, and once you got in, you "snap out of it" and couldn't recall a thing about the drive? Your automatic pilot kicked in and did the driving for you, and that's pretty handy, isn't it?

Hassle is, your brain didn't expand one little bit on that press home. As a matter of fact, it likely constricted a bitty bit instead. How about next time, you say to yourself "I'm going to try a fresh road home, simply for the fun of it". What could occur? Well, first of all your automatic pilot is off, so you're utilizing your conscious brain driving home.

2nd, who knows what you might find on that fresh route? A fresh eating place you haven't tried? A re-modeled shop that might interest you? Another coffee shop than the one you constantly go to in the morning?

Well, I believe you get the picture. "Must I keep driving that fresh road?" you inquire. No, naturally not, unless you like it better. The point is that you tried something fresh today. You changed your brain in a little way, and that makes it grow.

Moreover, once you decide to try fresh fun things, who knows what lively fresh individuals you might meet along the way?

The sample above speaks more about the mental attitude you picked out, than the modest decision to take a fresh road home. You see, once you begin making minor changes, it gets to be a habit, which leads to greater shifts.

Those greater shifts may lead to all sorts of fantastic things for you. You'll see more serendipity, creative thinking and passion in your life; you'll formulate a more outgoing personality and attempting fresh fun things may open the door to meet fresh lively individuals.

In time, this may all build self-assurance and self-regard, and bring expanded happiness and significance to your life. You'll be believing less "I can't do that", and more "Well, simply perhaps I may!"

Chapter 4:

Synopsis

If you're plunked down on a sofa or chair right now, encircled by 4 walls and a ceiling, you're not solo. In fact, this is the #1 anti-activity — seated disease. It's the top reason more and more of us have no passion. Our progressively homebound, car-bound, office-bound, computer-bound life-style takes up a lot of our lives.

Do Something Different

This isn't what our bodies or brains were built for. For the huge majority of humankind's history, we spent our days doing outside forcible labor. Our sedentary life-style is a fresh arrival —but we've surely accepted it!

Convenience might be good, but lack of daily action isn't. Sedentary living has been associated to every major health disorder of our times: as well as lack of passion.

Get outside! Switch off the television, push the ottoman away from the couch, lace your shoes and get outdoors for at least half-hour a day, plus a couple of hours every weekend.

Sure, we understand, you don't have to go outside to get a great workout.

But simply looking at flowers alleviates depression and sparks creativity.

There's no research to affirm it, but it makes intuitive sense that time spent outside adds to good health, higher relaxation, more fitness, or more passion. After all, whether you're walking, gardening, biking, or simply getting the mail, being outside inherently means becoming more active than being indoors. It's not on any medical group's prescribed recommendations, but we say, make 'more time outside' among your top passion-improvement goals.

Here are thoughts to help you accomplish just that:

Get on outside clothes the minute you come home from work. For many of us, work-clothing is inside clothes. Make it a ritual: arrive home, right away switch into a tee shirt and shorts, and begin the 2nd part of your day anew.

Hold crucial gear by the door. Outside shoes, dark glasses, a brimmed hat, sun block, and bug repellent all are crucial summer outside gear. Have them all prepared in the same place by your back entrance.

Match eating time with outside time. Dinner took twenty minutes? Then walk for twenty minutes outside right away after eating.

Garden in little batches. Most of us lay aside gardening jobs for the weekend. The result: many hours of difficult work, the last few not really fun. Alternatively, garden in 30-minute spurts all week long.

This will get you outside more often, and you'll never get bored or fatigued as of the brevity of the job. Best of all, come the weekend, your yard and garden will require only a little work, leaving you more time for play!

Adopt more nature walks. If you've adopted walking as part of your regimen, fantastic!

Put together a toy box. What do you love doing outside? Whether it's golfing, rehearsing your fishing fly casting, doing watercolors, shooting basketballs, playing badminton, playing with your dog, have your gear in a bin near your back entrance, ready for instant use.

Chapter 5:

Get Creative

Synopsis

There's a huge myth in our civilization: that passion may solely be spontaneous. You either like your job or you do not. You either like working out or detest it. You're interested in reading books or you find them awful. That passion can't be coerced or produced.

I take issue. Passion may be produced. Even for things you do not presently like.

By fine-tuning the activities and pastimes you engage in, you may discover a passion for anything. All it takes is a little patience and an open brain.

Changing It

The advantage is that you wind up loving the things you have to do anyways. Working out, learning, reading, working and nearly any pursuit might be made into a passion.

And if you understand how to do it, existent passions may be turned from gently interesting to energizing. The skill of discovering your passion is like turning up the dial for the quantity of color you have in life. Here are a few ways to find your passion:

Curiosity is the cornerstone of passion. Cast off your present intellects and start from the view that you're almost totally ignorant on the subject. Then seek novelty to boost your interest.

Make it a contest - supply yourself rules, objectives and strategical restraints. The more originative thinking required, the greater.

Put together a particular goal along with a deadline. This might infuse routine actions with a sense of direction and purpose. Publishing a report goes from being only another job, to an originative challenge that promotes you.

Find hidden chances for self-expression. This might mean inventing a style for folding up clothes. Switching the format you compose code in or altering the style of your presentment. View every activity as an act of expression and originality.

Cut down distractions and get rid of noise. The more you center on an activity the better you might notice interesting qualities about it. The only really boring activity is the one you can't pay attention to.

Discover ways to utilize skills you already have in a fresh endeavor. An artistic individual could draw images to help himself study. An athletic individual may be able to utilize her strength and endurance as a speaker.

If an action is too hard for you to become enthusiastic about it, slow up. Worry less about outcomes and more about experimenting till you develop skill.

Energy is catching. If you spend time with somebody who exudes passion about a matter, some of it will rub off on you. Seek out individuals who have the energy you want and get them to distinguish their motivation. Frequently it will point you to key data you had no idea might be so interesting.

For awful tasks, make them harder. For frustrating jobs, make them simpler. This might be done by altering the speed or restraints you require to complete a job.

Boring jobs might be made more interesting by adjusting a time-limit. Frustrative assignments might be made simpler by allowing yourself an awful first-draft rather than perfection.

- 23 -

Confidence is essential for passion, but arrogance might destroy it. Build a humble self-assurance where you trust in your abilities to handle the strange, but you likewise have a great respect for it.

Chapter 6:

Synopsis

Is school straining you ? Is work annoying you? We all have to have time to ourselves. Even if you're not strained, taking time to be by yourself may be calming and rewarding.

Great Info

Make certain that everything else is in check. Even if you're strained or tired, make sure that your house is orderly, so as not to let things prey on you beware while you're enjoying a minute to yourself.

Climb in a bath.

- As you fill the bathtub, add a few bubbles to the running water.
- While waiting, read a magazine to pass the time.
- Light a few scented candles.
- Dim the lights and get into the tub.
- Shut your eyes and unwind.
- Free your brain of any worries. Remove yourself from the rest of the Earth for the next 30 minutes.

Unwind and enjoy yourself.

- Prepare a pet snack. Enjoy a relaxing herb tea.
- Watch an old film.
- Read a short story.
- Daydream.
- Contemplate.
- Take a long snooze.

- Do zip.

Living with your mind centered on the future causes you to miss out on the here and now and our lives are made out of seconds of now, not of seconds of the future. By living in the future you don't really live at all.

Naturally, it'd be nice to live so I'm trying to love the journey – the present. Here are a few ways to accomplish that:

Pure centering is bliss. When your thoughts, behaviors and emotions are all directed toward an individual function you're centering and you're in the present. You ought to get lost in your work. Set a deadline for yourself to complete a task and see your level of centering skyrocket.

Two of my acquaintances and I meet up every now and again to discuss business, thoughts, and just random stuff really. It's reasonably flexible and unprofessional, however we still label it as a organize session.

Although the very construct of a organize session is centered on acquiring results in the future I feel there's likewise a sense of living in the here and now, as we all simply sit around a table or outdoors on the grass and talk. There's no fancy technology, really little note taking and it's simply pure discussion. And possibly most especially: its fun.

Time flies. Find like-minded people and put your heads together.

Being in a hurry doesn't give you an opportunity to appreciate the present. I realize there are assorted apparent urgencies you might feel in your life. I find taking things slower and merely being patient more rewarding.

Slow down the speed of life.

When you introduce balance into your life you get mindful of what you're doing, giving you an opportunity to acknowledge seconds for what they are: precious gifts of chronology. Don't let anything devour your life.

Realize what you want the future to hold and set a plan to oblige that. This gives you perhaps the most potent tool in accomplishment: certainty.

Wrapping Up

If you trust in something, are passionate about it and may see the end result so clearly that you may taste it, you feel certain that it's inevitable. You're no longer questioning if, but when. And this is powerful.

With this certainty you are able to quit stressing over what might or might not occur in the future because there's merely no wondering – you're going to accomplish it and that's final. Accomplishment merely becomes a matter of doing X to accomplish Y.

This might seem like a cold way to approach life, however when the outcome Y is understood, every moment X may be fully appreciated as they aren't bombarded by self-distrust or doubt. You may live in the present because your future becomes a predetermined (but still open to spontaneousness) mass of wonder.

Set a direction for your life and love the ride.